MW01116443

# In Celebration Of

_____

**Date :** _____

**Time :** _____

**Place :** _____

Guest Name : ......................................................................

# Baby Predictions

Gender : .......................... Weight : ..........................

Name Suggestion : ...........................................

Date Of Birth : ................................................

Time Of Birth: ................................................

Height : ............................................

Hair Color : .........................................

# Advice For Parents

..................................................................................................................

..................................................................................................................

..................................................................................................................

..................................................................................................................

# Wishes For Baby

..................................................................................................................

..................................................................................................................

..................................................................................................................

..................................................................................................................

*Welcome Little One*

Guest Name : .................................................................

# Baby Predictions

Gender : ..................... Weight : .....................

Name Suggestion : .................................

Date Of Birth : .........................................

Time Of Birth: .........................................

Height : .........................................

Hair Color : .........................................

# Advice For Parents

..............................................................................

..............................................................................

..............................................................................

..............................................................................

# Wishes For Baby

..............................................................................

..............................................................................

..............................................................................

..............................................................................

*Welcome Little One*

**Guest Name :** ..........................................................

# Baby Predictions

**Gender :** ........................ **Weight :** ........................

**Name Suggestion :** ........................................

**Date Of Birth :** ............................................

**Time Of Birth:** ............................................

**Height :** ........................................

**Hair Color :** ........................................

# Advice For Parents

.......................................................................

.......................................................................

.......................................................................

.......................................................................

# Wishes For Baby

.......................................................................

.......................................................................

.......................................................................

.......................................................................

Welcome Little One

Guest Name : ........................................................

# Baby Predictions

Gender : ........................... Weight :.........................

Name Suggestion : ...................................

Date Of Birth :......................................................

Time Of Birth:......................................................

Height :...............................................

Hair Color :...............................................

# Advice For Parents

..............................................................................................................

..............................................................................................................

..............................................................................................................

..............................................................................................................

# Wishes For Baby

..............................................................................................................

..............................................................................................................

..............................................................................................................

..............................................................................................................

*Welcome Little One*

Guest Name : .................................................................

# Baby Predictions

Gender : ........................ Weight : ........................

Name Suggestion : .................................................

Date Of Birth : ...........................................................

Time Of Birth : ...........................................................

Height : ...............................................................

Hair Color : ............................................................

# Advice For Parents

..............................................................................................

..............................................................................................

..............................................................................................

..............................................................................................

# Wishes For Baby

..............................................................................................

..............................................................................................

..............................................................................................

..............................................................................................

*Welcome Little One*

Guest Name : ................................................................

Advice For Parents

# Baby Predictions

Gender : ......................... Weight : .........................

Name Suggestion : ...............................................

Date Of Birth : .......................................................

Time Of Birth: .......................................................

Height : ..............................................

Hair Color : ...............................................

# Advice For Parents

..........................................................................................................

..........................................................................................................

..........................................................................................................

..........................................................................................................

# Wishes For Baby

..........................................................................................................

..........................................................................................................

..........................................................................................................

..........................................................................................................

*Welcome Little One*

Guest Name : ...............................................................

# Baby Predictions

Gender : ...................... Weight : ......................

Name Suggestion : ...............................................

Date Of Birth : .......................................................

Time Of Birth: ........................................................

Height : ...............................................

Hair Color : .............................................

# Advice For Parents

..............................................................................

..............................................................................

..............................................................................

..............................................................................

# Wishes For Baby

..............................................................................

..............................................................................

..............................................................................

..............................................................................

*Welcome Little One*

Guest Name : ........................................................................

# Baby Predictions

Gender : ................................ Weight : ........................

Name Suggestion : ...............................................

Date Of Birth : ...................................................

Time Of Birth : ...................................................

Height : ..............................................

Hair Color : ..............................................

# Advice For Parents

..................................................................................................

..................................................................................................

..................................................................................................

..................................................................................................

# Wishes For Baby

..................................................................................................

..................................................................................................

..................................................................................................

..................................................................................................

*Welcome Little One*

Guest Name : ..................................................................

# Baby Predictions

Gender : ............................ Weight :.........................

Name Suggestion : .......................................

Date Of Birth :..........................................................

Time Of Birth:..........................................................

Height :.........................................

Hair Color :...........................................

# Advice For Parents

...........................................................................................

...........................................................................................

...........................................................................................

...........................................................................................

# Wishes For Baby

...........................................................................................

...........................................................................................

...........................................................................................

...........................................................................................

*Welcome Little One*

Guest Name : .......................................................

# Baby Predictions

Gender : ........................ Weight : ........................

Name Suggestion : ........................................

Date Of Birth : ...............................................

Time Of Birth: ...............................................

Height : ..............................................

Hair Color : ...........................................

# Advice For Parents

..................................................................................................

..................................................................................................

..................................................................................................

..................................................................................................

# Wishes For Baby

..................................................................................................

..................................................................................................

..................................................................................................

..................................................................................................

*Welcome Little One*

Guest Name : .............................................................

# Baby Predictions

Gender : ...................................... Weight : ........................

Name Suggestion : ......................................................

Date Of Birth : ...........................................................

Time Of Birth: ...........................................................

Height : ..................................................

Hair Color : ..................................................

# Advice For Parents

........................................................

........................................................

........................................................

........................................................

# Wishes For Baby

........................................................

........................................................

........................................................

........................................................

*Welcome Little One*

Guest Name : ...............................................................................

# Baby Predictions

Gender : ............................ Weight : ........................

Name Suggestion : ........................................

Date Of Birth : ............................................................

Time Of Birth: ............................................................

Height : ............................................

Hair Color : ............................................

# Advice For Parents

......................................................................................

......................................................................................

......................................................................................

......................................................................................

# Wishes For Baby

......................................................................................

......................................................................................

......................................................................................

......................................................................................

Welcome Little One

Guest Name : ....................................................................

# Baby Predictions

Gender : ......................... Weight : .........................

Name Suggestion : ......................................

Date Of Birth : ..............................................................

Time Of Birth .............................................................

Height : .................................................

Hair Color : .................................................

# Advice For Parents

..................................................................................................

..................................................................................................

..................................................................................................

..................................................................................................

# Wishes For Baby

..................................................................................................

..................................................................................................

..................................................................................................

..................................................................................................

Welcome Little
One

Guest Name : .....................................................

# Baby Predictions

Gender : ........................... Weight :.........................

Name Suggestion : ...................................

Date Of Birth : ...............................................

Time Of Birth:................................................

Height : ................................................

Hair Color :................................................

# Advice For Parents

..................................................................................

..................................................................................

..................................................................................

..................................................................................

# Wishes For Baby

..................................................................................

..................................................................................

..................................................................................

..................................................................................

*Welcome Little One*

Guest Name : .....................................................

# Baby Predictions

Gender : ..................... Weight : ......................

Name Suggestion : .............................

Date Of Birth : .....................................................

Time Of Birth: .....................................................

Height : ...............................................

Hair Color : ...............................................

# Advice For Parents

...........................................................................................................

...........................................................................................................

...........................................................................................................

...........................................................................................................

# Wishes For Baby

...........................................................................................................

...........................................................................................................

...........................................................................................................

...........................................................................................................

*Welcome Little One*

Guest Name : ..................................................

# Baby Predictions

Gender : ........................ Weight : ................

Name Suggestion : .................................

Date Of Birth : ...........................................

Time Of Birth: ...........................................

Height : ..................................

Hair Color : ..................................

# Advice For Parents

..................................................................................................................

..................................................................................................................

..................................................................................................................

..................................................................................................................

# Wishes For Baby

..................................................................................................................

..................................................................................................................

..................................................................................................................

..................................................................................................................

Welcome Little One

Guest Name : .....................................................

# Baby Predictions

Gender : ...................... Weight : ......................

Name Suggestion : .........................................

Date Of Birth : ................................................

Time Of Birth: ................................................

Height : ...................................

Hair Color : ......................................

# Advice For Parents

..........................................................................

..........................................................................

..........................................................................

..........................................................................

# Wishes For Baby

..........................................................................

..........................................................................

..........................................................................

..........................................................................

*Welcome Little One*

**Guest Name :** ..................................................................

# Baby Predictions

**Gender :** ........................... **Weight :** ......................

**Name Suggestion :** ...........................................

**Date Of Birth :** ............................................................

**Time Of Birth:** ............................................................

**Height :** ...............................................

**Hair Color :** ...........................................

# Advice For Parents

..................................................................................

..................................................................................

..................................................................................

..................................................................................

# Wishes For Baby

..................................................................................

..................................................................................

..................................................................................

..................................................................................

Welcome Little One

Guest Name : ....................................................

# Baby Predictions

Gender : ........................ Weight :........................

Name Suggestion : ................................

Date Of Birth :........................................

Time Of Birth:........................................

Height :........................................

Hair Color :........................................

# Advice For Parents

..............................................................................................

..............................................................................................

..............................................................................................

..............................................................................................

# Wishes For Baby

..............................................................................................

..............................................................................................

..............................................................................................

..............................................................................................

Welcome Little One

Guest Name : ................................................

# Baby Predictions

Gender : ........................ Weight : ..................

Name Suggestion : ...............................

Date Of Birth : ......................................

Time Of Birth: ......................................

Height : ...........................................

Hair Color : ........................................

# Advice For Parents

..................................................................................................................

..................................................................................................................

..................................................................................................................

..................................................................................................................

# Wishes For Baby

..................................................................................................................

..................................................................................................................

..................................................................................................................

..................................................................................................................

*Welcome Little One*

Guest Name : ................................................................

# Baby Predictions

Gender : ........................ Weight : ........................

Name Suggestion : ....................................

Date Of Birth : ....................................

Time Of Birth: ....................................

Height : ....................................

Hair Color : ....................................

# Advice For Parents

..............................................................................

..............................................................................

..............................................................................

..............................................................................

# Wishes For Baby

..............................................................................

..............................................................................

..............................................................................

..............................................................................

*Welcome Little One*

Guest Name : .............................................................

# Baby Predictions

Gender : ........................ Weight : .......................

Name Suggestion : ...............................

Date Of Birth : ..........................................

Time Of Birth: ..........................................

Height : ................................................

Hair Color : ............................................

# Advice For Parents

..................................................................................................

..................................................................................................

..................................................................................................

..................................................................................................

# Wishes For Baby

..................................................................................................

..................................................................................................

..................................................................................................

..................................................................................................

*Welcome Little One*

**Guest Name :** ........................................................

# Baby Predictions

**Gender :** ........................... **Weight :** ...........................

**Name Suggestion :** ...................................................

**Date Of Birth :** ...................................................

**Time Of Birth :** ...................................................

**Height :** ...................................................

**Hair Color :** ...................................................

# Advice For Parents

..................................................................................

..................................................................................

..................................................................................

..................................................................................

# Wishes For Baby

..................................................................................

..................................................................................

..................................................................................

..................................................................................

Welcome Little One

Guest Name : ....................................................................

# Baby Predictions

Gender : ......................... Weight :.........................

Name Suggestion : .................................

Date Of Birth :..............................................

Time Of Birth:..............................................

Height : .........................................

Hair Color :.........................................

# Advice For Parents

..............................................................................

..............................................................................

..............................................................................

..............................................................................

# Wishes For Baby

..............................................................................

..............................................................................

..............................................................................

..............................................................................

*Welcome Little One*

Guest Name : ................................................................

## Baby Predictions

Gender : ............................ Weight : ........................

Name Suggestion : ................................................

Date Of Birth : ......................................................

Time Of Birth: ......................................................

Height : ..............................................

Hair Color : ..........................................

# Advice For Parents

..................................................................

..................................................................

..................................................................

..................................................................

# Wishes For Baby

..................................................................

..................................................................

..................................................................

..................................................................

*Welcome Little One*

Guest Name : ..................................................................

# Baby Predictions

Gender : ......................... Weight :.........................

Name Suggestion : ...........................................

Date Of Birth :..............................................................

Time Of Birth:..............................................................

Height : .............................................

Hair Color :.............................................

# Advice For Parents

..............................................................................................

..............................................................................................

..............................................................................................

..............................................................................................

# Wishes For Baby

..............................................................................................

..............................................................................................

..............................................................................................

..............................................................................................

Welcome Little One

Guest Name : ..................................................

# Baby Predictions

Gender : ........................ Weight :..................

Name Suggestion : ..............................

Date Of Birth :......................................

Time Of Birth:......................................

Height :............................................

Hair Color :........................................

# Advice For Parents

..................................................................................................

..................................................................................................

..................................................................................................

..................................................................................................

# Wishes For Baby

..................................................................................................

..................................................................................................

..................................................................................................

..................................................................................................

*Welcome Little One*

**Guest Name :** ............................................................

# Baby Predictions

**Gender :** ........................ **Weight :** ........................

**Name Suggestion :** ........................................

**Date Of Birth :** ........................................

**Time Of Birth:** ........................................

**Height :** ........................................

**Hair Color :** ........................................

# Advice For Parents

...................................................................................

...................................................................................

...................................................................................

...................................................................................

# Wishes For Baby

...................................................................................

...................................................................................

...................................................................................

...................................................................................

*Welcome Little One*

Guest Name : .......................................................................

# Baby Predictions

Gender : ...........................  Weight : ........................

Name Suggestion : ..................................

Date Of Birth : ....................................................

Time Of Birth: ....................................................

Height : ...................................................

Hair Color : ................................................

# Advice For Parents

..............................................................................................

..............................................................................................

..............................................................................................

..............................................................................................

# Wishes For Baby

..............................................................................................

..............................................................................................

..............................................................................................

..............................................................................................

Welcome Little One

Guest Name : ..............................................................

# Baby Predictions

Gender : ...................... Weight :.....................

Name Suggestion : ....................................

Date Of Birth :...........................................

Time Of Birth:...........................................

Height : ....................................

Hair Color :....................................

# Advice For Parents

........................................................................

........................................................................

........................................................................

........................................................................

# Wishes For Baby

........................................................................

........................................................................

........................................................................

........................................................................

*Welcome Little One*

Guest Name : ..................................................................

# Baby Predictions

Gender : ........................ Weight : ........................

Name Suggestion : ..............................................

Date Of Birth : ......................................................

Time Of Birth: .....................................................

Height : ...............................................

Hair Color : ..............................................

# Advice For Parents

..................................................................................................

..................................................................................................

..................................................................................................

..................................................................................................

# Wishes For Baby

..................................................................................................

..................................................................................................

..................................................................................................

..................................................................................................

Welcome Little One

Guest Name : ....................................................

# Baby Predictions

Gender : ..........................  Weight :....................

Name Suggestion : .....................................

Date Of Birth :..........................................

Time Of Birth:...........................................

Height :.................................

Hair Color :.............................

# Advice For Parents

..............................................................................................

..............................................................................................

..............................................................................................

..............................................................................................

# Wishes For Baby

..............................................................................................

..............................................................................................

..............................................................................................

..............................................................................................

*Welcome Little One*

Guest Name : .....................................................

# Baby Predictions

Gender : .......................... Weight : ...................

Name Suggestion : .................................

Date Of Birth : ...........................................

Time Of Birth : ..........................................

Height : ..................................................

Hair Color : ..............................................

# Advice For Parents

........................................................................................

........................................................................................

........................................................................................

........................................................................................

# Wishes For Baby

........................................................................................

........................................................................................

........................................................................................

*Welcome Little One*

Guest Name : ....................................................

# Baby Predictions

Gender : ........................... Weight : ...................

Name Suggestion : ...............................

Date Of Birth : .........................................

Time Of Birth: ........................................

Height : ...........................................

Hair Color : ......................................

# Advice For Parents

..................................................................................................

..................................................................................................

..................................................................................................

..................................................................................................

# Wishes For Baby

..................................................................................................

..................................................................................................

..................................................................................................

..................................................................................................

Welcome Little One

**Guest Name :** ....................................................

# Baby Predictions

**Gender :** ........................ **Weight :** ........................

**Name Suggestion :** ........................................

**Date Of Birth :** ..........................................

**Time Of Birth:** ..........................................

**Height :** ..........................................

**Hair Color :** ..........................................

# Advice For Parents

......................................................................

......................................................................

......................................................................

......................................................................

# Wishes For Baby

......................................................................

......................................................................

......................................................................

......................................................................

*Welcome Little One*

Guest Name : ...................................................................

# Baby Predictions

Gender : ...........................  Weight : ........................

Name Suggestion : ...................................................

Date Of Birth : ............................................................

Time Of Birth: ...........................................................

Height : ......................................................

Hair Color : ..........................................

# Advice For Parents

..........................................................................................

..........................................................................................

..........................................................................................

..........................................................................................

# Wishes For Baby

..........................................................................................

..........................................................................................

..........................................................................................

..........................................................................................

Welcome Little One

**Guest Name :** ....................................................................

# Baby Predictions

**Gender :** ........................... **Weight :** ...........................

**Name Suggestion :** ...................................................

**Date Of Birth :** .........................................................

**Time Of Birth:** .........................................................

**Height :** ...................................................

**Hair Color :** ...................................................

# Advice For Parents

..................................................................................................

..................................................................................................

..................................................................................................

..................................................................................................

# Wishes For Baby

..................................................................................................

..................................................................................................

..................................................................................................

..................................................................................................

Welcome Little One

Guest Name : .............................................................

# Baby Predictions

Gender : ...........................  Weight :.........................

Name Suggestion : ...........................................

Date Of Birth :...........................................................

Time Of Birth:...........................................................

Height : ...............................................

Hair Color :...............................................

# Advice For Parents

..................................................................................................

..................................................................................................

..................................................................................................

..................................................................................................

# Wishes For Baby

..................................................................................................

..................................................................................................

..................................................................................................

..................................................................................................

Welcome Little One

Guest Name : ...........................................................

# Baby Predictions

Gender : ....................... Weight : .......................

Name Suggestion : ...................................

Date Of Birth : ..........................................

Time Of Birth: .........................................

Height : ..................................

Hair Color : .................................

# Advice For Parents

......................................................................................................

......................................................................................................

......................................................................................................

......................................................................................................

# Wishes For Baby

......................................................................................................

......................................................................................................

......................................................................................................

......................................................................................................

*Welcome Little One*

Guest Name : .......................................................................

# Baby Predictions

Gender : ......................... Weight : .........................

Name Suggestion : .........................................

Date Of Birth : .............................................

Time Of Birth: ................................................

Height : ....................................................

Hair Color : ..............................................

# Advice For Parents

..................................................................................................

..................................................................................................

..................................................................................................

..................................................................................................

# Wishes For Baby

..................................................................................................

..................................................................................................

..................................................................................................

..................................................................................................

*Welcome Little One*

Guest Name : ...........................................

# Baby Predictions

Gender : ........................ Weight : ........................

Name Suggestion : ...........................................

Date Of Birth : ...........................................

Time Of Birth: ...........................................

Height : ...........................................

Hair Color : ...........................................

# Advice For Parents

......................................................................................................

......................................................................................................

......................................................................................................

......................................................................................................

# Wishes For Baby

......................................................................................................

......................................................................................................

......................................................................................................

......................................................................................................

*Welcome Little One*

Guest Name : ...........................................................

# Baby Predictions

Gender : ........................ Weight : ........................

Name Suggestion : ................................................

Date Of Birth : ................................................

Time Of Birth: ................................................

Height : ........................................

Hair Color : ....................................

# Advice For Parents

..................................................................................................

..................................................................................................

..................................................................................................

..................................................................................................

# Wishes For Baby

..................................................................................................

..................................................................................................

..................................................................................................

..................................................................................................

*Welcome Little One*

Guest Name : ........................................................

# Baby Predictions

Gender : ........................ Weight : ........................

Name Suggestion : ........................................

Date Of Birth : ........................................

Time Of Birth: ........................................

Height : ........................................

Hair Color : ........................................

# Advice For Parents

..................................................................................................

..................................................................................................

..................................................................................................

..................................................................................................

# Wishes For Baby

..................................................................................................

..................................................................................................

..................................................................................................

..................................................................................................

*Welcome Little One*

Guest Name : ...........................................................

# Baby Predictions

Gender : ....................... Weight : ......................

Name Suggestion : .................................

Date Of Birth : ...................................................

Time Of Birth: ..................................................

Height : ...............................................

Hair Color : ............................................

# Advice For Parents

....................................................................................

....................................................................................

....................................................................................

....................................................................................

# Wishes For Baby

....................................................................................

....................................................................................

....................................................................................

....................................................................................

*Welcome Little One*

Guest Name : ..............................................................

# Baby Predictions

Gender : ............................ Weight : ...........................

Name Suggestion : ...................................

Date Of Birth : ...........................................

Time Of Birth: ............................................

Height : .......................................

Hair Color : .........................................

# Advice For Parents

........................................................................................................

........................................................................................................

........................................................................................................

........................................................................................................

# Wishes For Baby

........................................................................................................

........................................................................................................

........................................................................................................

........................................................................................................

*Welcome Little One*

Guest Name : ...........................................

# Baby Predictions

Gender : ..................... Weight : ...................

Name Suggestion : ................................

Date Of Birth : .....................................

Time Of Birth: .....................................

Height : .................................

Hair Color : .................................

# Advice For Parents

..................................................................................................

..................................................................................................

..................................................................................................

..................................................................................................

# Wishes For Baby

..................................................................................................

..................................................................................................

..................................................................................................

..................................................................................................

*Welcome Little One*

**Guest Name :** ............................................................

# Baby Predictions

**Gender :** ........................ **Weight :** ........................

**Name Suggestion :** ........................................

**Date Of Birth :** ................................................

**Time Of Birth:** ................................................

**Height :** ................................................

**Hair Color :** ................................................

# Advice For Parents

..................................................................................................

..................................................................................................

..................................................................................................

..................................................................................................

# Wishes For Baby

..................................................................................................

..................................................................................................

..................................................................................................

..................................................................................................

*Welcome Little One*

Guest Name : ..............................................................

# Baby Predictions

Gender : ............................ Weight : ......................

Name Suggestion : ...........................................

Date Of Birth : ..................................................

Time Of Birth: ..................................................

Height : .............................................

Hair Color : ..........................................

# Advice For Parents

...............................................................................................

...............................................................................................

...............................................................................................

...............................................................................................

# Wishes For Baby

...............................................................................................

...............................................................................................

...............................................................................................

...............................................................................................

Welcome Little One

Guest Name : ..................................................................................................

# Baby Predictions

Gender : ...................................... Weight : ....................................

Name Suggestion : ..............................................................

Date Of Birth : .........................................................................

Time Of Birth: ...........................................................................

Height : .........................................................................

Hair Color : .........................................................................

# Advice For Parents

..........................................................................................

..........................................................................................

..........................................................................................

..........................................................................................

# Wishes For Baby

..........................................................................................

..........................................................................................

..........................................................................................

..........................................................................................

*Welcome Little One*

**Guest Name :** ..................................................................

# Baby Predictions

**Gender :** ........................... **Weight :** ...........................

**Name Suggestion :** ...............................................

**Date Of Birth :** .....................................................

**Time Of Birth:** .....................................................

**Height :** ...............................................

**Hair Color :** ...............................................

# Advice For Parents

..........................................................................................................

..........................................................................................................

..........................................................................................................

..........................................................................................................

# Wishes For Baby

..........................................................................................................

..........................................................................................................

..........................................................................................................

..........................................................................................................

Welcome Little
One

Made in the USA
Middletown, DE
24 August 2024

59670252R00057